HOMEMADE Dog Food COOK BOOK

Easily Prepare
Healthy Biscuits, Snacks & Meals

Brenda L. Blake

NOTE TO READERS

This dog food recipe book is filled with healthy recipes for biscuits, snacks and kibble replacement meals. The recipes that I share in this book are based on my personal experience and the extensive research I have done over the years, while showing and breeding Kennel Union of South Africa (KUSA) registered dogs.

This dog food recipe book is the perfect gift for dog lovers who are passionate about maintaining the long-term health of their pets.

For the dog-lovers who are interested in obtaining more in-depth information about canine nutrition, please refer to the US Department of Agriculture (USDA) FoodData Central Website.

About the Author

I gained a basic knowledge of cooking methods many years ago, when I completed a Cordon Bleu Diploma in Paris. Subsequently I returned to live in South Africa and qualified as a Food Safety Auditor. I have been breeding Kennel Union of South Africa (KUSA) registered dogs as a hobby, for more than 40 years. I feed my furry family only the highest quality kibble with 32% protein content as their main meal, supplemented with healthy homemade biscuits, treats and kibble replacement meals. I have never had any obese dogs, and over the past 30+ years, none of my dogs has developed a chronic illness.

My kennel was recently showcased by the magazine Pets24 "as a testament to four decades of dedication and excellence in breeding miniature schnauzers. With a focus on producing healthy and happy pups."

I sincerely hope that you will find the recipes included in this book to be economical, simple to prepare, and beneficial in assuring the long-term happiness and health of your pets.

DISCLAIMER

The insights and recipes that I share in this book are based on my personal experience and the extensive research I have done over the years, while showing and breeding Kennel Union of South Africa (KUSA) registered dogs.

By using the recipes and guidance notes in this book you acknowledge and accept responsibility for your pet's safety and health on the understanding that the author is not liable for any adverse effects or outcomes resulting from the use of the information provided.

Consult with your veterinarian for guidance if you have any questions or concerns regarding your pet's health or safety.

Copyright © 2026 by Brenda L. Blake

All rights reserved.

It is not legal to duplicate, reproduce or transmit any part of this document in printed form or electronic means. It is strictly prohibited to record this publication and any storage of this document without the written consent of the publisher or author except for brief quotes in a book review.

TABLE OF CONTENTS

NOTE TO READERS 1

DISCLAIMER 2

1. HEALTHY DOG BISCUIT RECIPES 7

    Recipes For Healthy Dog Biscuits 8

    Recipe For Simple Dog Biscuits 9

    Misty's Healthy Oatmeal Biscuits 11

    Healthy Sweet Potato & Butternut Dog Biscuits 13

    Carrot & Sunflower Seed Crunchies 15

    Pumpkin & Sweet Potato Biscuits 19

    Healthy Peanut Butter Biscuits 17

2. RECIPES FOR HEALTHY TREATS & SNACKS 20

    Healthy Turkey Snacks 21

    Healthy Beef Liver Snacks 25

    Chewy Carrot Treats 23

    Sweet Potato Treats 27

    Butternut And Thyme Snacks 28

3. HEALTHY EGG-BASED SNACKS 29

    Healthy Eggs With Chicken Livers Snack 30

    Misty's Best Egg-Toasty Bites 31

    Healthy Egg & Brown Rice Snack 33

    Healthy Baked Egg & Carrot Custard 35

Egg And Cauliflower Bake 37

MESSAGE FROM BRENDA L BLAKE 38

4. HEALTHY RECIPES WITH TUNA & HAKE 39

Misty's Favorite Tuna & Quinoa Extravaganza 40

Hake With Vegetables And Couscous 40

Hake And Rice Casserole 43

Tuna With Pasta 44

Hake With Butternut & Rice 45

5. HEALTHY GELATINE-BASED TREATS & HELPFUL TIPS 46

Chicken & Butternut Chewy Treats 50

Carrot Flavor Chewy Treats 53

Beef Flavor Chewy Treats 55

Minty Fresh Breath Chewy Treats 48

Pumpkin Flavor Chewy Treats 57

6. RECIPES FOR HEALTHY FRUIT & VEGGIE SNACKS & HELPFUL TIPS.59

Health Benefits 61

7. HEALTHY RECIPES WITH CHICKEN OR TURKEY BREAST 63

Quick & Easy Chicken Broth 66

Chicken Or Turkey Breast With Rice 68

Chicken Or Turkey Breast With Veggies 70

Chicken Or Turkey Breast With Veggies And Couscous 71

Chicken Or Turkey Breast With Pasta 71

Chicken Or Turkey Breast Quinoa Bake 72

8. HEALTHY MEALS WITH PORK OR BEEF MINCE 75

- Mince & Veggie Medley With Rice 77
- Mince With Oats, Carrots And Cabbage 78
- Tinker's Yummy Mince & Butternut With Rice 79
- Mince, Veggies And Pasta Bake 80
- Mince Baked With Veggies And Quinoa 81
- Mince With Veggies And Couscous 83
- Mince & Veggie Hotpot 84

9. RECIPES FOR HEALTHY MEALS WITH LEAN BEEF OR CHICKEN HEART 85

- Beef Heart With Veggies And Couscous 87
- Beef Heart, Veggies and Pasta 87
- Beef & Veggie Extravaganza 88
- Tinker's Best Beef & Veggie Casserole 91

10. HEALTHY KIBBLE REPLACEMENT RECIPES WITH CHICKEN GIBLETS 92

- Bruno's Chicken Licken Giblets & Veggies 94
- Slow-Cooked Chicken Giblets With Couscous 95
- Misty's Favorite Chicken Giblets And Quinoa Bake 96
- Chicken Giblets Or Necks And Veggies With Rice 97
- Chicken Giblets And Pasta Extraordinaire 98

11. HEALTHY KIBBLE REPLACEMENT MEALS – WITH LAMB 99

- Homemade Mutton Marrow Bone Broth 101
- Teddy's Best Lamb And Quinoa Bowl 102

Lamb And Pasta Bake 103

Teddy's Favorite Lamb Shoulder & Veggie Fiesta 105

Lamb Heart With Carrots, Peas And Rice 104

Lamb With Couscous And Veggies 107

12. HEALTHY KIBBLE REPLACEMENT RECIPES COOKED WITH LIVER 108

Liver Extravaganza With Quinoa 110

Liver With Couscous 111

Snoopy's Favorite Liver & Veggies 112

Liver And Pumpkin Medley With Rice 113

Liver & Veggie Hotpot 114

13. HELPFUL TIPS - FOODS TO AVOID AND FOODS SAFE TO EAT 115

14. TIPS ON TRAINING YOUR DOG WITH HEALTHY REWARD-TREATS & SNACKS 120

REFERENCES 123

1. HEALTHY DOG BISCUIT RECIPES

Lucy's favorite dog biscuits

RECIPES FOR HEALTHY DOG BISCUITS

What's included:

1. Recipe for Simple Dog Biscuits
2. Misty's Healthy Oatmeal Biscuits
3. Healthy Sweet Potato & Butternut Dog Biscuits
4. Carrot & Sunflower Seed Crunchies
5. Healthy Peanut Butter Biscuits
6. Pumpkin and Sweet Potato Biscuits

Easy to prepare and relatively inexpensive

Your pets will enjoy devouring these healthy biscuits. The ingredients are relatively inexpensive, and the recipes are simple to prepare.

To prevent the biscuits from going moldy, store in an airtight container, or keep refrigerated or frozen.

Health Benefits for Dogs

These delicious dog biscuits are packed with proteins, vitamins and minerals needed by every dog to keep their bones, coat, skin and nails healthy. Be aware, some dogs may be allergic to some of the ingredients, for example, peanut butter + eggs. If your dog is prone to allergies, consult your veterinarian before introducing new foods.

> **Note:** The US Department of Agriculture (USDA) FoodData Central Website (fdc.nal.usda.gov) provides detailed information on the nutritional values of all of the listed ingredients. You will find it interesting and most informative.

Ingredient Conversion Quantities

Conversion quantities recorded for ingredients have been rounded to approximate equivalents.

RECIPE FOR SIMPLE DOG BISCUITS

Ingredients

- 3 eggs
- ½ cup (1 small) chopped sweet potato
- 1 cup (250 ml) water
- 1/2 cup (180ml) sunflower oil
- 2½ cups (375g) whole wheat flour
- 2 cups (240g) white bread flour
- 1 Tbsp (10g) unflavoured gelatine

Instructions

1. Place the chopped raw sweet potato and water in a microwave proof bowl. Microwave for 5 minutes.
2. Drain the water and set aside.
3. Combine sweet potato, oil, and eggs in a blender. Liquidize to form a puree.
4. Combine the flour and gelatine in a mixing bowl. Mix well. Add the puree. Mix well.
5. If needed, add a little water to gather up any dry bits to form a soft, but not too sticky dough. (or add a little flour to form a soft dough).
6. Place the dough on a lightly floured surface. Cover and leave to rest for 10 minutes, then roll out approximately 3mm thick ($1/4$ inch) on a lightly floured surface.
7. Use a 2 inch (4 cm) cookie cutter to cut the dough into biscuits. Then place each biscuit on a lightly greased and floured baking pan. Prick lightly with a fork.
8. Preheat the oven to 180 C (350F).

9. Bake the biscuits for 20-25 minutes or until lightly browned. Cool on a rack. Pack into airtight containers or Ziplock bags.

Storage

Once cool, store biscuits in Ziplock bags in freezer until ready to eat. Remove one bag at a time, and once defrosted, store in refrigerator, for 1 week max.

MISTY'S HEALTHY OATMEAL BISCUITS

Ingredients

- 4 cups (380g) rolled oats
- 1 cup (120g) white bread flour
- 4 eggs
- 1 cup (250 ml) water
- 1/3 cup (80 ml) sunflower oil
- 1 tbsp unflavored gelatine

Instructions

1. Blend the rolled oats in a blender till fine. Then turn into a mixing bowl.
2. Mix in the eggs, oil, water and gelatine and white bread flour to form a smooth dough.
3. Turn the dough onto a lightly floured surface.
4. If needed, add a little additional water to gather up any dry bits to form a soft, but not too sticky dough (or alternatively, add a little white bread flour to form a soft dough).
5. Cover and leave to rest for 5 minutes, then roll out approximately 3mm thick ($1/4$ inch) on a lightly floured surface.
6. Use a 2 inch (4 cm) cookie cutter to cut the dough into biscuits. Then place each biscuit on a lightly greased and floured baking pan.
7. Prick lightly with a fork.
8. Preheat the oven to 180 C (350F)
9. Bake the biscuits for 25 minutes or until lightly browned. Cool on a rack. Pack into airtight containers or Ziplock bags.

Storage

Once cool, store biscuits in Ziplock bags in freezer until ready to eat. Remove one bag at a time, and once defrosted, store in refrigerator, for 1 week max.

Misty's Healthy Oatmeal Biscuits

HEALTHY SWEET POTATO & BUTTERNUT DOG BISCUITS

Ingredients

- 1 cup (140g) chopped butternut
- ½ cup (1 small) chopped sweet potato
- 350ml water
- 3 eggs
- ½ cup (120ml) sunflower oil
- 3 cups (360g) whole wheat flour
- 1 cup (120g) white bread flour

Instructions

1. Place the chopped raw butternut, sweet potato and water in a microwave proof bowl. Microwave for 5 minutes.
2. Drain the water and set aside.
3. Combine the butternut, sweet potato, oil, and eggs in a blender. Liquidize to form a puree.
4. Combine the flour in a mixing bowl. Mix well. Add the puree.
5. If needed, add a little water to gather up any dry bits to form a soft, but not too sticky dough. (or add a little water to form a soft dough)
6. Place the dough on a lightly floured surface. Cover and leave to rest for 10 minutes, then roll out approximately 3mm thick ($1/4$ inch) on a lightly floured surface.
7. Use a 2 inch (4 cm) cookie cutter to cut the dough into biscuits. Then place each biscuit on a lightly greased and floured baking pan. Prick lightly with a fork.
8. Preheat the oven to 180 C (350F). Bake the biscuits for 25 minutes or until lightly browned. Cool on a rack. Pack into airtight containers or Ziplock bags.

Storage

Once cool, store biscuits in Ziplock bags in freezer until ready to eat. Remove one bag at a time, and once defrosted, store in refrigerator, for 1 week max.

CARROT & SUNFLOWER SEED CRUNCHIES

Ingredients

- 1 cup (150g) carrots chopped
- 1/2 cup (1 small) sweet potato chopped
- 1 cup (250 ml) water
- 2½ cups (375g) whole wheat flour
- 2 cups (240g) white bread flour
- 3 eggs
- ½ cup (120ml) sunflower oil
- ½ cup (70g) shelled sunflower seeds

Instructions

1. Place the chopped raw carrots, sweet potato, and water in a microwave proof bowl. Microwave for 5 minutes on medium heat. Drain the water.
2. In a blender, combine the carrots, sweet potato, eggs and oil. Liquidize to form a smooth puree. Turn the mixture into a mixing bowl.
3. Add the flour and sunflower seeds.
4. Mix well. If needed, add a little water to gather up any dry bits to form a soft, but not too sticky dough.
5. Use a rolling pin to roll the dough approximately 3 mm thick ($^1/_4$ inch) on a lightly floured surface.
6. Use a cookie cutter to cut the dough into biscuits. Then place each biscuit on a lightly greased and floured baking pan.
7. Preheat the oven to 180C (350F)
8. Bake the biscuits for 25 minutes or until lightly browned. Cool on a rack.

Storage

Store crunchies in an airtight container in the refrigerator for 2 weeks max. or freeze for 3 months max.

PUMPKIN & SWEET POTATO BISCUITS

Ingredients

- 1 cup (250g) chopped raw pumpkin
- $1/2$ cup (70g) shelled sunflower seeds
- $1/2$ cup (1 small) sweet potato chopped
- 1 cup (250ml) water
- 3 cups (360g) whole wheat flour
- 1 cup (120g) white bread flour
- 4 eggs
- ½ cup (125ml) sunflower oil

Instructions

1. Place the chopped raw pumpkin, sweet potato and water in a microwave proof bowl. Microwave for 5 minutes on medium heat. Drain the water.
2. In a blender, combine the pumpkin, sweet potato, eggs and oil. Liquidize to form a smooth puree. Turn the mixture into a mixing bowl.
3. Add the flour and raw, shelled sunflower seeds.
4. Mix well. If needed, add a little water to gather up any dry bits to form a soft, but not too sticky dough (or if needed, add a little extra flour to form a soft dough.
5. Use a rolling pin to roll the dough approximately 3 mm thick ($1/4$ inch) on a lightly floured surface.
6. Use a cookie cutter to cut the dough into biscuits. Then place each biscuit on a lightly greased and floured baking pan.
7. Preheat the oven to 180C (350F).

8. Bake the biscuits for 25 minutes or until lightly browned. Cool on a rack.

Storage

Store cookies in an airtight container in the refrigerator for 2 weeks max. or freeze for 3 months max.

HEALTHY PEANUT BUTTER BISCUITS

Ingredients

- 4 tbsp (60g) natural smooth peanut butter (no added salt or sugar)
- 4 eggs
- 1½ cups (375ml) water.
- 2½ cups (375g) whole wheat flour
- 2 cups (240g) white bread flour

Be aware: Peanut allergies in dogs are rare. Best to consult your veterinarian before giving peanut butter if your dog has allergies

Instructions

1. In a mixing bowl, combine the eggs, peanut butter and water. Mix well.
2. Stir in the flour.
3. Add more water if needed, to make soft, but not too sticky dough.
4. Use a rolling pin to roll the dough approximately 3 mm thick ($^1/_4$ inch) on a lightly floured surface.
5. Use a 4 cm (2 inch) cookie cutter to cut the dough into biscuits. Then place each biscuit on a lightly greased and floured baking pan.
6. Preheat the oven to 180 C (350F).
7. Bake the biscuits for 20-25 minutes or until lightly browned. Cool on a rack.

Storage

Store cookies in an airtight container in the refrigerator for 2 weeks max. or freeze for 3 months max.

2. RECIPES FOR HEALTHY TREATS & SNACKS

What's included:

1. Healthy Turkey Snacks
2. Healthy Beef Liver Snacks
3. Chewy Carrot Treats
4. Sweet Potato Treats
5. Butternut and Thyme Snacks

Affordable and easy to prepare

These treats and snacks are affordable, and the recipes are easy to prepare.

To prevent these treats and snacks from going moldy, they must be stored in an airtight container. Refrigerate or freeze immediately.

Health Benefits for Dogs

Treats and snacks are intended as rewards and should make up maximum 5% of your dog's daily food intake.

Be aware that some dogs may be allergic to some of the ingredients, for example, flour. Consult your veterinarian before introducing new foods If your dog is prone to allergies.

> **_Note:_** *The US Department of Agriculture (USDA) FoodData Central Website (https://fdc.nal.usda.gov) provides detailed information on the nutritional values of all the listed ingredients. You will find it interesting and most informative.*

Ingredient Conversion Quantities

Conversion quantities recorded for ingredients have been rounded to approximate equivalents.

HEALTHY TURKEY SNACKS

Ingredients

- 500g semi-frozen turkey (or chicken) breasts
- 3 tbsp (45ml) vegetable oil

Note: *Be aware that some dogs may be allergic to poultry (turkey & chicken)*

Instructions

1. Slice the turkey breasts thinly, along the grain, approximately ½ cm (¼ inch) thick and place in a small mixing bowl.
2. Add the oil, and mix well, to coat the turkey strips with oil.

Option 1: Lightly grease the air fryer basket

3. Lay the turkey strips in the air fryer basket.
4. Bake 5 minutes at 180C (350F) then reduce the temperature to 160C (250F)
5. Bake for approximately 30 minutes, then flip over the turkey strips. Reduce heat to 120C (250F) and bake for a further 10 minutes or until crisp.

Option 2: Preheat the oven to 160C (325F)

3. Lightly grease a cake rack and place on a backing tray.
4. Lay the turkey strips on the lightly greased cake rack
5. Bake 15 minutes at 160C then flip over the chicken strips
6. Reduce the temperature to 120C (250F) and bake until crisp, approximately 2½ hours, depending on size of the chicken strips.

Storage

Once cool, store turkey strips in an airtight container in the **refrigerator** for 1 week max. or **freeze** for 3 months max.

Treats made from turkey or chicken breasts should not provide more than 5% of your dog's daily food intake.

Healthy Turkey Snacks

HEALTHY BEEF LIVER SNACKS

Ingredients

- 400g chopped raw beef liver
- 1 cup (1 medium) chopped sweet potato
- 1 cup (250ml) water
- 4 eggs
- ½ cup (125ml) sunflower oil
- 4 cups (520g) whole wheat flour
- $2^1/_2$ cups (310g) white bread flour
- 2 tbsp (20g) unflavored gelatine

Instructions

1. Place the chopped raw sweet potato and water in a microwave proof bowl. Microwave for 6 minutes on medium heat (or until soft).
2. Drain the water and set aside.
3. Combine the raw beef liver, sweet potato, oil, and eggs in a blender. Liquidize to form a puree.
4. Combine the whole wheat flour, white bread flour and gelatine in a mixing bowl. Mix well. Add the beef liver puree.
5. If needed, add a little water to gather up any dry bits to form a soft, but not too sticky dough.

Baking

6. Mix well, then turn the dough into a lightly floured surface and knead for 2 minutes.

7. Turn the dough into a greased and lightly floured 14 x 7 inch (36 cm x 26cm) baking pan.
8. Preheat the oven to 180C (350F).
9. Bake for 1 hour. Turn onto a rack to cool.
10. Cut into Bite Sized Cubes. Use a bread knife to cut the 'cake' into bite sized cubes.

Storage

Refrigerator 1 week max.

Freezer: Half-fill small plastic or Ziplock bags with cookies, and store in the freezer max.3 months. Defrost one bag at a time. Keep refrigerated till ready to serve.

CHEWY CARROT TREATS

Ingredients

- 4 medium carrots
- 1 tbsp (15 ml) sunflower oil
- 1 tsp (3g) dried thyme

Instructions

1. Peel the carrots then cut each carrot in half. Cut each half carrot lengthwise into thin strips.
2. Place the carrot strips in a bowl and coat with oil. Sprinkle with thyme. Mix well.
3. Preheat the oven to 160C (325F)
4. Lay the carrot strips on a lightly greased baking tray.
5. Bake for 45 minutes at 160C (325F).
6. Reduce the temperature to 120C (250F) and bake until crisp, approximately 1-2 hours, depending on size of carrot strips. Cool on a rack.

Storage

Store treats in an airtight container in the **refrigerator** for maximum 1 week. **Freezer** Storage max. 3 months.

Chewy Carrot Snacks

SWEET POTATO TREATS

Ingredients

- 2 cups (400g) peeled sweet potatoes
- ¼ cup (60ml) sunflower oil
- 1 tsp (5ml) oreganum

Instructions

1. Slice the sweet potatoes into discs, approximately ½ cm ($1/8$ inch) thick.
2. Place in a bowl and add the sunflower oil. Mix well to coat with oil.
3. Sprinkle with oreganum.

Option 1: Pre-heat Air fryer.

4. Lay the sweet potato discs in the air fryer basket.
5. Bake 15 minutes at 160C (325F) then reduce the temperature to 120C (250F)
6. Bake until crisp, for approximately 30 minutes depending on size of discs.

Option 2: Preheat the oven to 160C (325F)

4. Lay the sweet potato discs on a lightly greased baking tray.
5. Bake 10 minutes at 160C then flip the discs over.
6. Reduce the temperature to 120C (250F) and bake until crisp, approx. 2-3 hours, depending on size of discs. Cool on a rack.

Storage

Store cookies in an airtight container in the **refrigerator** for 1 week max. or **freeze** for 3 months max.

BUTTERNUT AND THYME SNACKS

Ingredients

- 1 cup (200g) butternut
- 2 tbsp (30 ml) vegetable oil
- ½ tsp thyme

Instructions

1. Slice the butternut into discs, approx. 3cm (1/8 inch) thick.
2. Combine the oil and thyme in a bowl. Mix well. Leave to infuse for 10 minutes
3. Add the thinly sliced butternut discs and mix well, to coat with oil.

Option 1: Pre-heat Air fryer.

4. Lay the butternut discs flat (don't overlap) in air fryer basket.
5. Bake at 120C (250F) for 30 minutes or until crisp, depending on the size of the discs.
6. Cool on a rack.

Option 2: Preheat the oven to 160C (325F)

4. Lay the butternut discs on a lightly greased baking tray.
5. Bake 10 minutes at 160C then flip the discs over.
6. Reduce the temperature to 120C (250F) and bake until crisp, approximately 2-3 hours, depending on size of discs.
7. Cool on a rack.

Storage

Store treats in an airtight container in the **refrigerator** for maximum 1 week. **Freezer** Storage max. 3 months.

3. HEALTHY EGG-BASED SNACKS

What's included:

1. Healthy Egg with Chicken Liver Snack
2. Misty's Best Egg-Toasty Bites
3. Healthy Egg & Brown Rice Snack
4. Healthy Egg & Carrot Custard
5. Egg & Cauliflower Bake

Affordable and convenient

Easily prepare these inexpensive and highly nutritious egg-based snacks using ingredients you already have in your kitchen. Your pets will enjoy every mouthful.

Health Benefits for Dogs

Ideally, give your dog at least 1 -2 eggs a week. Eggs are rich in protein, vitamins, minerals and fatty acids every dog needs to stay healthy and live a good life.

Be aware: Some dogs may be allergic to eggs. If your dog is prone to allergies, consult your veterinarian before introducing egg-based foods.

> **Note:** *The US Department of Agriculture (USDA) FoodData Central Website (https://fdc.nal.usda.gov) provides detailed information on the nutritional values of all of the listed ingredients. You will find the website interesting and most informative.*

Ingredient Conversion Quantities

Conversion quantities recorded for ingredients have been rounded to approximate equivalents.

HEALTHY EGGS WITH CHICKEN LIVERS SNACK

Ingredients

- 4 eggs
- 1 cup (125g) cooked chopped chicken livers
- 10g (20ml) corn flour
- 80ml (1/3 cup) milk
- 1 tbsp (10ml) sunflower oil

Instructions

1. Pre-heat the oven to 180°C.
2. Combine the milk and corn flour in a measuring cup. Mix until smooth.
3. Whisk the eggs in a mixing bowl. Add the milk and corn flour and mix well.
4. Stir in the chopped cooked chicken livers.
5. Grease an ovenproof baking dish with sunflower oil.
6. Turn the eggs and chicken livers into the baking dish.
7. Bake for 45 minutes or until a skewer comes out clean
8. Turn onto a plate and leave to cool. Cut into slices.

Refrigerator Storage

Store leftovers covered in the refrigerator max.3 days.

Serving Suggestion

Give each dog 1-2 slices a day until there is no more left.

MISTY'S BEST EGG-TOASTY BITES

Ingredients

- 2 eggs
- ½ cup (125ml) milk
- 1 tbsp (10g) corn flour
- 4 slices of whole wheat brown bread
- 1 tbsp finely chopped parsley
- 1/4 cup (60 ml) sunflower oil

Instructions

1. Cut the bread into quarters.
2. Combine the milk and corn flour in a bowl. Whisk in the eggs.
3. Soak the bread in the egg mixture.
4. Heat 1 tbsp oil in a frying pan. Fill the pan with egg-soaked bread.
5. Cook for 2 minutes each side or until lightly browned.
6. Turn onto a plate and allow to cool while cooking the remaining slices of bread.

Refrigerated storage

Store leftovers in an airtight container in the refrigerator max. 3 days.

Serving Suggestion

Give each dog 1-2 toasty bites a day until there are no more left. Add a few slices of cucumber as additional treats.

Misty's Best Egg-Toasty Bites

HEALTHY EGG & BROWN RICE SNACK

Ingredients

- 4 eggs
- 1 tbsp heaped (15 g) corn flour
- 2 tbsp (40ml) milk
- 1 cup (180g) cooked brown rice
- ¼ cup brown breadcrumbs
- 1 tbsp (15ml) sunflower oil

Instructions

1. Combine the eggs, milk and corn flour in a mixing bowl.
1. Add the cooked rice and mix well.
2. Heat the oil in a frying pan.
3. Turn spoonfuls of the mixture into the frying pan. Sprinkle with breadcrumbs.
4. Cook on low heat for 2 minutes. Then flip over and cook for a further 1-2 minutes until cooked through.
5. Turn onto a plate. Cut into bite sized snacks.
6. Then repeat until there is no mixture left.
7. Allow to cool before serving.

Refrigerated storage

Store leftovers in an airtight container in the refrigerator max. 3 days.

Serving Suggestion

Give each pet 3 bite sized snacks a day until there are no more left.

Healthy Egg and Brown Rice Snack

HEALTHY BAKED EGG & CARROT CUSTARD

Ingredients

- 3 eggs
- 1½ tbsp (15g) corn flour
- 1½ cups (360 ml) milk
- 1 medium cooked carrot cubed
- 1 tbsp (15g) butter or margarine

Instructions

1. In a microwave proof measuring cup microwave 1 cup of milk for 1 minute.
2. Mix the corn flour with ½ cup milk until smooth stir into the warm milk.
3. Whisk the eggs in a mixing bowl. Add the milk and corn flour and mix well.
4. Stir in the cooked carrot cubes.
5. Pour the mixture into a well buttered microwave proof baking dish.
6. Cover and microwave for 7-8 minutes on medium heat or until set.
7. Cool for 30 minutes before serving.

Note: *If you overcook the custard, it may separate.*
The dogs will love eating it anyway.

Refrigerated storage

Store leftovers covered in the refrigerator max. 3 days.

Serving Suggestion

Give each dog 1-2 spoonfuls of baked egg custard a day until there is no more left.

> **Note**: *Some dogs are lactose intolerant. My dogs are not lactose intolerant, and I have been preparing this baked egg custard for my dogs for more than 30 years.*

EGG AND CAULIFLOWER BAKE

Ingredients

- 4 eggs
- 1 cup (150g) steamed cauliflower chopped
- ½ cup (125ml) milk
- 1 tablespoon (10g) cornflour
- 1 tbsp (10g) unflavored gelatine
- 1 tbsp (15g) butter or margarine
- ¼ cup (35g) grated cheese

Instructions

1. Preheat the oven to 180C (350F).
2. Whisk the milk and corn flour in a bowl. Add the eggs.
3. Add the chopped cauliflower and mix well.
4. Turn the mixture into a well buttered ovenproof baking dish.
5. Sprinkle with grated cheese. Then bake for 8-10 minutes until lightly browned.
6. Cool for 30 minutes before serving.

Refrigerator Storage

Store leftovers covered in the refrigerator max. 3 days.

Serving Suggestion

Give each dog 1-2 spoonfuls of egg and cauliflower bake until there is no more left.

MESSAGE FROM BRENDA L BLAKE

I hope your furry family are devouring these healthy treats and meals with gusto, and that you've enjoyed this homemade dog food recipe book as much as I've enjoyed creating them. Your feedback (via a review on Amazon) is really important to me. It will help me shape my next book.

If you've found this book worthwhile, please take a couple of moments to share a review with Amazon.

You can do this by:

1. Checking the book's page on Amazon or locating it through your purchase.
2. Scrolling to the bottom of the page and clicking on the 'Customer Review' button
3. Leaving a rating out of 5 or writing a brief review to share your experience.

Warm regards

4. HEALTHY RECIPES WITH TUNA & HAKE

What's included:

1. Misty's Favorite Tuna & Quinoa Extravaganza
2. Hake with Veggies and Couscous
3. Hake and Rice Casserole
4. Tuna with Pasta
5. Hake with Butternut and Rice

Easy to prepare recipes

These healthy fish-based recipes are easy to prepare and inexpensive.

Caution for Dogs with Allergies

If your dog is prone to allergies, consult your Vet before introducing new foods.

Be aware, some dogs may be allergic to some of the ingredients, for example, fish.

> *Note:* *The US Department of Agriculture (USDA) FoodData Central Website (fdc.nal.usda.gov) provides detailed information on the nutritional values of all the listed ingredients. You will find the website interesting and most informative.*

Ingredient Conversion Quantities

Conversion quantities recorded for ingredients have been rounded to approximate equivalents.

MISTY'S FAVORITE TUNA & QUINOA EXTRAVAGANZA

Ingredients

- 1 small tin (170 g) Tuna in water
- 100g (2 medium) carrots sliced
- 1 cup (1 small) sweet potato diced
- 2 cups (500ml) water
- 1 cup (180g) quinoa
- 1 tbs (15ml) vegetable oil

Instructions

1. Preheat the oven to 180C (350F)
2. In a mixing bowl, mix the tuna, carrots, sweet potato, and oil.
3. Turn the mixture into an ovenware baking dish. Add the water and quinoa.
4. Cover and bake for 30 minutes on low heat. Stir well. Bake for a further 5 minutes or until all the liquid is absorbed.
5. Allow to cool before serving.

Refrigerated Storage

Store leftovers covered for maximum 1 week in refrigerator.

Freezer Storage

Store in freezer-safe containers or Ziplock bags for max. 3 months. Once defrosted, store in the refrigerator.

HAKE WITH VEGETABLES AND COUSCOUS

Ingredients

- 500g raw hake sliced
- 1½ cups (210g) butternut diced
- 1 cup (150g) peas
- 1½ cups (375ml) water
- 1 cup (190g) couscous.
- 12ml (2 tbs) sunflower oil

Note: Some dogs may be allergic to fish and/or the gluten in couscous. If your dog is prone to allergies, consult your veterinarian.

Instructions

1. In a saucepan combine the hake, oil and water. Bring to a boil.
2. Add the vegetables and cook on medium for 20 minutes. Stir well.
3. Stir the couscous into the hot mixture, then switch off the heat, cover and leave for 15 minutes to absorb the liquid. Stir well.
4. Allow to cool 30 minutes before serving.

Refrigerated Storage

Store leftovers covered for maximum 1 week in refrigerator.

Freezer Storage

Store in freezer-safe containers or Ziplock bags max. 3 months.

Hake with vegetables and couscous

HAKE AND RICE CASSEROLE

Ingredients

- 750g sliced hake.
- 1 cup (135g) carrots diced
- 1 cup (90g) chopped broccoli chopped
- 2 cups (500ml) boiling water
- 1 cup brown rice
- 1/3 cup (80ml) sunflower oil

Instructions

1. In a bowl mix the hake, carrots, broccoli and oil.
2. Turn the mixture into an ovenproof baking dish. Add the water and brown rice. Mix well.
3. Cover and bake for 45 minutes.
4. Cool for 30 minutes before serving.

Note: *Some dogs may be allergic to fish. If your dog is prone to allergies, consult your veterinarian before introducing cooked fish.*

Refrigerated Storage

Store leftovers covered for maximum 1 week in refrigerator.

TUNA WITH PASTA

Ingredients

- 1 small tin (170g) tuna in water.
- 1 cup (135g) diced butternut
- 1 cup (90g) chopped broccoli chopped
- 2 cups (500ml) boiling water
- 1 cup (100 gm) macaroni
- 1/3 cup (80ml) sunflower oil

Instructions

1. In a bowl mix the tuna, butternut, broccoli and oil.
2. Turn the mixture into an ovenproof baking dish. Add the boiling water.
3. Cover and bake for 30 minutes.
4. Stir the macaroni into the hot mixture. Bake for a further 15 minutes. Stir well.
5. Cool 30 minutes before serving.

Refrigerated Storage

Store leftovers covered for maximum 1 week in refrigerator.

HAKE WITH BUTTERNUT & RICE

Ingredients

- 750g sliced hake.
- 1 cup (140g) butternut diced
- 1 cup (90g) peas
- 2 cups (500ml) boiling water
- 1 cup of brown rice
- 1/3 cup (80ml) sunflower oil

Instructions

1. In a bowl mix the hake, butternut, peas and oil.
2. Turn the mixture into an ovenproof baking dish. Add the water and brown rice. Mix well.
3. Cover and bake for 45 minutes.
4. Cool for 30 minutes before serving.

Refrigerated Storage

Store leftovers covered for maximum 1 week in refrigerator.

5. HEALTHY GELATINE-BASED TREATS & HELPFUL TIPS

What's included:

1. Carrot Flavor Chewy Treats
2. Beef Flavor Chewy Treats
3. Minty Fresh Breath Chewy Treats
4. Pumpkin Flavor Chewy Treats
5. Chicken and Butternut Chewy Treats

Quick and easy to prepare

Gelatine-based treats are made with homemade broth and gelatine. They're relatively inexpensive, and quick and easy to prepare using the homemade broth. In my experience, these chewy gelatine-based treats are the best treats to use for reward training purposes. My 'professional tasting team' (comprising Molly, Lucy, Misty and Teddy) enjoy the minty fresh-breath chewy treats as much as the other flavors.

Preparation

You can find unflavored gelatine at your local grocery store or health food shop. Prepare the broth used in the treats in advance. Refer to the homemade chicken broth (Chapter 7) and marrow bone broth (Chapter 11) recipes. If there is any mixture left over after filling the tray, set it aside and feed it to your dogs with a spoon.

Health Benefits for Dogs

Unflavored gelatine is made up of 85% collagen protein plus 12.3% Proline, an essential amino acid that builds protein. In addition, it is rich in minerals and vitamins.

These delicious treats will supplement your dog's daily meals with **protein, vitamins and minerals** needed to build a healthy coat, skin, bones and nails.

You can give your dog 2-3 gelatin treats each day to supplement their food. Be aware that some dogs may be allergic to some of the ingredients, for example, gelatine and eggs. If your dog is prone to allergies, consult your veterinarian before introducing new foods.

Note: *The US Department of Agriculture (USDA) FoodData Central Website (fdc.nal.usda.gov) provides detailed information on the nutritional values of all of the listed ingredients. You will find the website interesting and most informative.*

Treats should provide no more than 5% of your dog's daily food intake.

Ingredient Conversion Quantities

Conversion quantities provided for ingredients have been rounded to approximate equivalents.

CHICKEN & BUTTERNUT CHEWY TREATS

Ingredients

- ¼ cup (50g) chicken or turkey breast ground
- ½ cup (75g) butternut grated
- 1 cup (250ml) chicken broth
- 1 hard-boiled egg
- 5 tbsp (50g) unflavored gelatine

The addition of a wedge of hard-boiled egg provides B vitamins, vitamin D, Zinc, Copper, Iron.

Instructions

Give each dog 2-3 treats a day to supplement their food.

1. Place the raw ground chicken or turkey breast and chicken broth in a microwave safe dish. Add the butternut, cover and microwave on a medium heat for 5 minutes until cooked.
2. Sprinkle the gelatine into the hot mixture. Stir well.
3. Add sufficient boiling water to make up 2 cups (500ml).
4. Allow to cool for 15 minutes.
5. Spoon the mixture into a 36-cube silicone ice tray. Cover with shrink wrap. Allow to cool.
6. Then place in the refrigerator for approximately 4 ½ hours to set. Set any remaining mixture aside and feed to your dogs with a spoon.

Refrigerator Storage

Store covered for maximum 1 week in refrigerator.

Serving Suggestion

When ready to serve, pop each cube out of the silicone ice tray. For small dogs, cut each cube in half.

Serve with a wedge of hard-boiled egg.

CARROT FLAVOR CHEWY TREATS

Ingredients

- 2 cups (500ml) chicken broth
- 2 medium carrots grated
- 2 egg yolks
- 5 tbsp (50g) unflavoured gelatine
- ½ cup boiling water

Instructions

Give each dog 2-3 treats a day to supplement their food.

Option 1. Cook in Microwave

1. Place the chicken broth and carrots in a microwave safe measuring cup and microwave for 4 minutes on a medium heat or until soft.
2. Sprinkle the gelatine into the hot mixture. Stir well to dissolve the gelatine completely. Add sufficient boiling water to make up 375ml. Boil for one minute. Then allow to cool for 5 minutes.
3. Whisk the egg yolk into the hot mixture. Stir well.
4. Allow to cool for 25 minutes. Then follow step 5 below.

Option 2. Cook on Top of Stove

1. Place the chicken broth and carrots in a saucepan and cook on a medium heat for 6 minutes or until soft.
2. Sprinkle the gelatine into the hot mixture. Stir well to dissolve the gelatine completely. Add sufficient boiling water to make up 375ml. Boil for one minute. Then allow to cool for 5 minutes.
3. Whisk the egg yolk into the hot mixture. Stir well.

4. Allow to cool for 25 minutes. Then follow step 5 below.
5. Allow to cool for 30 minutes. Spoon the mixture into a 36-cube silicone ice tray. Cover with shrink wrap. Allow to cool. Then place in the refrigerator overnight to set.

Refrigerator Storage

Store covered for maximum 1 week in the refrigerator.

Serving Suggestion: When ready to serve, pop each cube out of the silicone ice tray. For small dogs, cut each cube in half.

Carrot flavored chewy treats

BEEF FLAVOR CHEWY TREATS

Ingredients

- 1¾ cups (375ml) beef marrow bone broth
- 2 egg yolks
- 4 tbsp (40g) unflavoured gelatine

Instructions

Give each dog 2-3 treats a day to supplement their food.

Cook on Top of Stove

1. In a saucepan, bring the beef marrow bone broth to boil on medium heat.
2. Sprinkle the gelatine powder into the broth and stir well. Simmer on low heat for 2 minutes. Stir well to dissolve completely. Switch off the heat. Cool for 5 minutes.
3. Whisk the egg yolk into the hot mixture. Stir well.
4. Allow to cool for 30 minutes.
5. Spoon the mixture into a 36-cube silicone ice tray. Cover with shrink wrap. Allow to cool. Then place in the refrigerator overnight to set.

Refrigerator Storage

Store covered for maximum 1 week in refrigerator.

Serving Suggestion

When ready to serve, pop each cube out of the silicone ice tray. For small dogs, cut each cube in half.

Beef Flavor Chewy Treats

MINTY FRESH BREATH CHEWY TREATS

Ingredients

- 10ml chopped fresh mint
- 1¾ cups (375ml) marrowbone broth (or chicken broth)
- 2 egg yolks
- 5 tbsp (50g) unflavoured gelatine

Instructions

Give each dog 2-3 treats a day to supplement their food and freshen breath. Your furry friends will beg for more!

Option 1. Cook in Microwave

1. In a small microwave safe measuring cup, combine mint and broth. Microwave covered for 3 minutes on medium.
2. Remove and discard the mint leaves.
3. Sprinkle the gelatine into the hot broth. Cook for 1 minute at medium heat. Stir well to dissolve gelatine completely. Allow to cool for 5 minutes
4. Whisk the egg yolks into the hot mixture.
5. Allow to cool for 30 minutes.
6. Spoon the mixture into a 36-cube silicone ice tray. Cover with shrink wrap. Allow to cool. Then place in the refrigerator overnight to set.
7. Set any remaining mixture aside and feed to your dogs with a spoon.

Option 2. Cook on Top of Stove

1. In a saucepan, combine chopped fresh mint leaves and broth. Bring to the boil. Simmer 5 minutes.
2. Remove and discard the mint leaves.
3. Sprinkle the gelatine into the hot broth Stir to dissolve. Allow to cool 10 minutes.
4. Whisk the egg yolks into the hot mixture. Stir well.
5. Allow to cool for 30 minutes.
6. Spoon the mixture into a 36-cube silicone ice tray. Cover with shrink wrap. Allow to cool. Then place in the refrigerator overnight to set.
7. Set any remaining mixture aside, and feed to your dogs with a spoon

Refrigerator Storage Store covered for maximum 1 week in refrigerator.

Serving Suggestion: When ready to serve, pop each cube out of the silicone ice tray. For small dogs, cut each cube in half.

PUMPKIN FLAVOR CHEWY TREATS

Ingredients

- 1$^1/_2$ cup (375ml) chicken broth
- $^1/_2$ cup (60g) pumpkin chopped
- ¼ cup (60ml) yogurt
- 1 tbsp (10g) ground flax/linseed
- 5 tbsp (50g) unflavoured gelatine

Instructions

Give each dog 2-3 treats a day to supplement their food.

Option 1. Cook in Microwave

1. Combine the chicken broth and chopped pumpkin in a microwave safe measuring cup.
2. Microwave on medium for 5 minutes. Stir well to dissolve completely. Cool for 5 minutes.
3. Then liquidize in a blender until smooth.
4. Sprinkle the gelatine into the hot mixture. Stir well to dissolve the gelatine completely. Microwave on medium for 30 seconds. Stir well.
5. Add the yogurt. Mix well.
6. Allow to cool for 30 minutes. Then follow Step 5 below.

Option 2. Cook on Top of Stove

1. In a saucepan, bring the chicken broth and grated pumpkin to the boil on medium heat. Cook for 5 minutes on low heat, stirring.
2. Sprinkle the gelatine powder into the broth and stir well. Simmer on low heat for 1 minute. Stir well to dissolve completely. Switch off the heat. Cool for 5 minutes. Then liquidize in a blender until smooth.
3. Whisk the yogurt into the hot mixture. Stir well.
4. Allow to cool for 30 minutes.
5. Spoon the mixture into a 36-cube silicone ice tray. Cover with shrink wrap. Allow to cool. Then place in the refrigerator overnight to set.

Refrigerator Storage

Store covered for maximum 1 week in refrigerator.

Serving Suggestion

When ready to serve, pop each cube out of the silicone ice tray. For small dogs, cut each cube in half.

6. RECIPES FOR HEALTHY FRUIT & VEGGIE SNACKS & HELPFUL TIPS

What's included:

1. Raw Apple Bites
2. Frozen Blueberries & Strawberries
3. Raw Butternut Bites
4. Raw Cucumber Slices
5. Raw Cauliflower Florets
6. Raw Carrot Slices
7. Raw Pumpkin Slices
8. Frozen Carrot Cubes

Relatively inexpensive, quick and easy to prepare

Your furry friends will love these inexpensive, easy to prepare and healthy fruit and vegetable snacks. The ingredients are relatively affordable, and the recipes are quick and simple.

Healthy fruit and veggie snacks are intended as rewards and not as kibble replacement meals.

Health Benefits for Dogs

The ingredients are packed with protein, vitamins, minerals and fiber needed to ensure long-term health and happiness. I have not included raw cherry tomatoes, although my own dogs love them, because some dogs may show an allergic reaction to raw tomatoes. If your dog is prone to allergies, consult your veterinarian before introducing new foods.

> **Note:** *The US Department of Agriculture (USDA) FoodData Central Website (fdc.nal.usda.gov) provides detailed information on the nutritional values of all the listed ingredients. You will find the website interesting and most informative.*

Ingredient Conversion Quantities

Conversion quantities recorded for ingredients have been rounded to approximate equivalents.

Health Benefits

SNACKS	INSTRUCTIONS	NUTRIENTS
Raw Apple Bites	Core the apple and slice into slices approx. ½ cm ($^1/_8$ inch) thick. Serve immediately.	Rich in Protein, Carbohydrate, Fiber, Minerals and Vitamins, including (but not limited to) Calcium, Magnesium, Phosphorus, Potassium, Vitamin C and Vitamin A.
Frozen Blueberries & Strawberries	Serve 3-4 frozen blueberries and/or strawberries as treats.	Rich In Carbohydrates, minerals and vitamins, including (but not limited to) calcium, magnesium, phosphorus, potassium and vitamin C.
Raw Butternut Bites	Slice the butternut into bite sized slices approximately ½ cm ($^1/_8$ inch) thick. Serve 2-3 slices as treats.	Rich in Protein, Carbohydrates, Fiber and Minerals, including (but not limited to) Calcium, Magnesium, Phosphorus, Potassium. Vitamins A & C.
Raw Cucumber Slices	Slice the cucumber into thin slices ½ 3cm ($^1/_8$ inch) thick. Give 3-4 slices as treats.	Carbohydrates, Minerals and Vitamins, including (but not limited to) Calcium, Magnesium, Phosphorus, Potassium. Choline, Vitamin K, Vitamin A.
Raw Cauliflower Florets	Cut the cauliflower into small florets. Give 1-3 florets as treats.	Protein, Carbohydrates, Vitamins and Minerals including (but not limited to), Calcium, Magnesium, Phosphorus, Potassium, Sodium, Vitamin C and Vitamin K.
Raw Carrot Slices	Excellent for cleaning teeth. Peel the carrots. Drop into boiling water for 30 seconds to release the beta carotene. Drain then cut each carrot into bite sized sticks or slices. Give 3-4 carrot sticks as treats.	Carbohydrates, Fiber, Minerals and Vitamins, including (but not limited to) Calcium, Magnesium, Phosphorus, Potassium, Iron, Vitamins A, K, C.

Raw Pumpkin Slices	Slice the pumpkin into bite sized slices ½ cm ($1/8$ inch) thick. Serve 2-3 slices as treats.	Protein Carbohydrates, Fiber, Minerals and Vitamins, Including (but not limited to) Calcium, Iron, Magnesium, Sodium, Phosphorus, Potassium, Vitamin A & C.
Frozen Carrot Cubes	Fill 32 cube silicone ice cube tray with 2 cups carrot juice. Freeze. When ready to serve, pop out one or two frozen cubes as treats.	Carbohydrates, Minerals and Vitamins, including (but not limited to) Calcium, Magnesium, Phosphorus, Potassium, Iron, Vitamins A, K, C.

The nutrients listed above for each ingredient have been summarized from the information published by the US Department of Agriculture (USDA) FoodData Central Website (https://fdc.nal.usda.gov/

7. HEALTHY RECIPES WITH CHICKEN OR TURKEY BREAST

Simple to prepare, relatively inexpensive

The recipes for healthy homemade meals that I have selected to share with you, are simple to prepare, relatively inexpensive; and assist in providing a nutritious diet for your dog.

Sourcing Everyday Ingredients

The ingredients selected are generally available at your local grocery store and in your own pantry. The ingredients have no added salt, sugar or preservatives, and have been selected based on the extensive research I have done on canine nutrition.

As an example, I have elected to include unflavored gelatine which contains 85% collagen protein, to supplement the protein content of many of the recipes.

If unflavored gelatine or any other ingredient is not available at your local grocery store, check at your local health food shop or online.

Portion sizes – A guideline only

The number of servings you will give your own dog to eat, will depend on the size and breed of your pet, and how active your dog is.

Portion sizes listed for healthy meals in this recipe book are a guideline only, based on the approximate quantity my own medium sized dogs eat at each meal. That is, approximately 3 heaped tablespoons (160g-180g) cooked food per dog for each kibble replacement meal. My dogs weigh between 7kg and 9kg.

As each dog is different, adjust the quantity you give your own dog, to meet your dog's specific needs.

Tips on Preparing Poultry Dishes

Try semi-freezing raw poultry before cutting into cubes. It is quicker and easier.

If your dog is prone to allergies

It is generally estimated that around 10% of dogs are prone to food allergies, for example, gluten contained in flour and various grains; and protein found in chicken, eggs, gelatine.

If your dog is prone to allergies, check with your veterinarian before changing your dog's diet.

What's included:

1. Recipe for Simple Chicken Broth
2. Chicken or Turkey Breast with Rice
3. Chicken or Turkey Breast with Veggies
4. Chicken or Turkey Breast and Veggies and Couscous
5. Chicken or Turkey Breast with Pasta
6. Chicken or Turkey Breast with Quinoa Bake

Readily available ingredients. Quick and easy to prepare and not expensive

Chicken or turkey breast is easily available and relatively inexpensive. Your four-legged friends will devour these delicious homemade meals and beg for more. Meals made with chicken and vegetables will supplement the food you feed your dog with nutritious proteins, vitamins and minerals every dog needs to maintain health.

Prepare the broth in advance

It is a good plan to prepare and freeze the broth in advance, as this will save time when preparing daily replacement meals.

Health Benefits

Chicken is a nutritious source of protein needed to build healthy coat, skin and bones.

Note: *Some dogs may be allergic to chicken and gelatine.*

Portion sizes – A guideline only

Each dog is different, and there is no hard and fast rule regarding how much your dog should eat. The number of servings you will give your dog to eat will depend on the size and breed of your pet, and how active your dog is.

QUICK & EASY CHICKEN BROTH

Ingredients

- 500g (½ kg) chicken necks
- 500g (½ kg) giblets
- 4 medium carrots chopped
- 3 celery stalks chopped
- ½ cup parsley chopped
- 8 cups (2 litres) water
- 2 tbsp (20g) unflavored gelatine.

Instructions

Option 1: Cook 20 minutes in Pressure Cooker

1. Place the chicken necks and giblets, prepared vegetables and water in saucepan.
2. Bring to the boil and simmer for 30 minutes on low heat.
3. Sprinkle the gelatine into the hot broth. Stir well to dissolve the gelatine completely. Proceed to step 4.

Option 2. Cook on top of the stove for 30 mins

1. In a saucepan, combined the raw necks and giblets, prepared vegetables, gelatine and boiling water.
2. Bring to the boil.
3. Simmer for 30 minutes on low heat.

Both options

4. Strain the broth into a measuring cup. Add sufficient water to make up 8 cups (2 liters) of broth.

5. Cover the broth and refrigerate.
6. Set aside the cooked necks, giblets and vegetables. Serve the giblets and necks as treats.
7. Your furry friend will enjoy the cooked vegetables as part of a meal.

Storage

Cool the broth then store in glass canning jars in refrigerator. Max.1 week. Freeze in freezer proof containers or Ziplock bags for maximum 3 months.

CHICKEN OR TURKEY BREAST WITH RICE

Ingredients

- 500g chicken or turkey breast chopped
- ½ cup (90g) rice
- 1 cup (135g) carrots sliced
- 1 cup (160g) green peas
- 1½ cups (375ml) broth
- 1 tbsp (10g) unflavored gelatine
- 1 tbsp (10ml) olive oil

Instructions

1. In a saucepan heat the oil then add the chicken or turkey breast Cook 5 minutes stirring, until lightly browned.
2. Add the rice, vegetables and broth.
3. Cover and cook 35 minutes on low heat. Stir well. Add more water if needed.
4. Allow to cool before serving.

Refrigerated Storage

Store leftovers covered for maximum 1 week in refrigerator.

Freezer Storage

Store in freezer-safe containers or Ziplock bags max. 3 months.

Chicken Breast with Veggies

CHICKEN OR TURKEY BREAST WITH VEGGIES

Ingredients

- 500g chicken or turkey breast chopped
- 1 cup (115g) pumpkin chopped
- ¾ cup (115g) raw sweet potato sliced
- ¾ cup (100g) carrots sliced
- ½ cup (75g) green beans chopped
- ½ cup (75g) red bell peppers chopped
- ½ cup (90g) zucchini sliced
- 1½ cups (375ml) chicken broth
- 1 tbsp (15ml) cooking oil

Instructions

1. Wash, peel and slice the raw vegetables.
2. In a saucepan, heat the oil, stir in the chicken or turkey breast and cook 5 minutes or until lightly browned.
3. Add the broth and bring to the boil.
4. Add the prepared vegetables, cover and simmer for 35 minutes, stir well.
5. Cool before serving.

Refrigerated Storage

Store leftovers for maximum 1 week in refrigerator.

Freezer Storage

Freeze in airtight contained for up to 3 months. Once defrosted, store in refrigerator for maximum
2 days.

CHICKEN OR TURKEY BREAST WITH VEGGIES AND COUSCOUS

Ingredients

- 500g chicken or turkey breast cut into cubes
- 1½ cups (175g) pumpkin diced
- 1 cup (150g) green beans chopped
- 1½ cups (375ml) broth
- 1 cup (190g) couscous.
- 12ml (2 tbsp) vegetable oil

Note: *Some dogs may be allergic to the gluten in couscous. If your dog is prone to allergies, consult your veterinarian.*

Instructions

1. In a saucepan add the oil and cubed chicken breast Cook for 5 minutes stirring. Then add the broth and bring to a boil.
2. Add the vegetables and cook on medium for 40 minutes. Stir well.
3. Stir the couscous into the hot mixture, then switch off the heat, cover and leave for 15 minutes to absorb the liquid. Stir well.
4. Allow to cool 30 minutes before serving.

Refrigerated Storage

Store leftovers covered for maximum 1 week in refrigerator.

Freezer Storage

Store in freezer-safe containers or Ziplock bags max. 3 months.

CHICKEN OR TURKEY BREAST WITH PASTA

Ingredients

- 500g chicken (or turkey breast) cubed.
- 1 cup (90g) chopped broccoli
- 1 cup (135g) diced carrots
- 2 cups (500ml) chicken broth
- 1 cup macaroni
- 10g (1 tbs) unflavored gelatine
- 25ml (1 tbs) vegetable oil

Instructions

1. In a saucepan heat the oil and cook the cubed chicken or turkey breast 5 minutes stirring, until lightly browned.
2. Turn the mixture into an ovenproof baking dish. Add the diced vegetables, and broth. Mix well.
3. Cover and bake for 30 minutes. Sprinkle the gelatine into the mixture.
4. Mix in the macaroni. Bake for a further 15 minutes. Stir well.
5. Cool 30 minutes before serving.

Refrigerated Storage

Store leftovers covered for maximum 1 week in refrigerator.

CHICKEN OR TURKEY BREAST AND QUINOA BAKE

Ingredients

- 500g chicken or turkey breast chopped
- 1 cup (150g) celery sliced
- 1 cup (150g) butternut diced
- 25g frozen green peas
- 2 cups (500ml) broth
- ¾ cup (135g) quinoa
- 10ml vegetable oil

Instructions

1. Preheat the oven to 180C (350F)
2. In a saucepan heat the oil then add the chopped chicken or turkey breast. Cook for 5 minutes stirring, until lightly browned.
3. Turn the mixture into an ovenware baking dish. Add the broth, quinoa and vegetables.
4. Cover and bake for 30 minutes on low heat. Stir well. Add the peas.
5. Bake for a further 5 minutes or until all the liquid is absorbed.
6. Allow to cool before serving.

Refrigerated Storage

Store leftovers covered for maximum 1 week in refrigerator.

Freezer Storage

Store in freezer-safe containers or Ziplock bags max. 3 months.

Turkey and Quinoa Bake

8. HEALTHY MEALS WITH PORK OR BEEF MINCE

What's included:

1. Mince & Veggie Medley with Rice
2. Mince with Oats, Carrots and Cabbage
3. Tinker's Yummy Mince & Butternut with Rice
4. Mince, Veggies & Pasta Bake
5. Mince Baked with Veggies and Quinoa
6. Mince with Veggies and Couscous
7. Mince & Veggie Hotpot

Quick and easy to make, using readily available ingredients.

Healthy meals made with beef and vegetables will supplement the food you feed your dog with the protein, vitamins and minerals every dog needs to maintain health and longevity. Your four-legged friends will love devouring these yummy, and relatively inexpensive kibble replacement meals made with lean beef.

To save time - Prepare the broth in advance

It is a good plan to prepare and freeze the broth in advance, as this will save time when preparing the kibble replacement meals.

Health Benefits

Beef is a nutritious source of protein needed to build healthy coat, skin, muscles, tendons and cartilage.

Note: Some dogs may be allergic to the protein in beef and gelatine.

Portion sizes – A guideline only

Portion sizes listed for healthy meals in this recipe book are a guideline only, based on the approximate quantity my own dogs eat at each meal. That is, approximately 160g -180g cooked food per kibble replacement meal. The number of servings you will give your own dog to eat will depend on the size and breed of your pet, and how active your dog is.

MINCE & VEGGIE MEDLEY WITH RICE

Ingredients

- 500g pork or beef mince
- 2 cups (270g) carrots sliced
- 1 cup (160g) green peas
- 1 cup (250ml) broth
- ½ cup (90g) rice
- 1 egg beaten
- 10g (1 tablespoon) unflavored gelatine
- 10ml olive oil

Instructions

1. In a saucepan heat the oil then add the mince. Cook for 5 minutes stirring, until lightly browned.
2. Add the carrots, rice and broth. Bring to the boil.
3. Sprinkle the gelatine into the broth. Mix well.
4. Cover and cook on medium heat for 30 minutes.
5. Stir the beaten egg into the hot mixture.
6. Add the peas and cook for 5 minutes or until all the liquid is absorbed. Stir well.
7. Cover and allow to cool before serving.

Refrigerated Storage

Store leftovers covered for maximum 1 week in refrigerator.

Freezer Storage

Store in freezer-safe containers or Ziplock bags for max. 3 months. Once defrosted, store in the refrigerator.

MINCE WITH OATS, CARROTS AND CABBAGE

Ingredients

- 500g pork or beef mince
- 2 cups (270 g) grated carrots
- 1 cup (150g) cabbage thinly shredded
- ¾ cup (70g) raw oats unflavored
- 1½ cups (375ml) broth
- 1 beaten egg
- 1 tbsp (15 ml) vegetable oil

Instructions

1. In a saucepan heat the oil and cook the mince for 5 minutes stirring, till lightly browned.
2. Turn the mixture into an ovenproof baking dish. Add grated vegetables, and broth. Mix well.
3. Cover and bake for 20 minutes.
4. Stir the beaten egg into the hot mixture.
5. Stir in the oats and bake for 5 minutes. Stir well.
6. Allow to cool 30 minutes before serving.

Refrigerated Storage

Store leftovers covered for maximum 3 days in refrigerator.

TINKER'S YUMMY MINCE & BUTTERNUT WITH RICE

Ingredients

- 500g pork or beef mince
- ½ cup (70g) butternut sliced
- ½ cup (90g) zucchini sliced
- ½ cup (80g) green peas
- 2 cups (500 ml) broth
- ½ cup (90g) rice
- 2 tbsp (25 ml) olive oil

Instructions

1. In a saucepan heat the oil then add the mince. Cook for 5 minutes stirring, until lightly browned.
2. Add vegetables, rice and broth.
3. Cover and cook 35 minutes on low heat. Stir well. Add more water if needed.
4. Allow to cool before serving.

Refrigerated Storage

Store leftovers covered for maximum 1 week in refrigerator.

Freezer Storage

Store in freezer-safe containers or Ziplock bags max. 3 months.

MINCE, VEGGIES AND PASTA BAKE

Ingredients

- 500g pork or beef mince
- ¾ cup (125g) celery chopped
- 1½ cups (200g) carrots diced
- 1 cup (180g) zucchini sliced
- 2 cups (500ml) broth
- 1 cup macaroni
- 1 tbsp (10g) unflavored gelatine
- 25ml (1 tbs) vegetable oil

Instructions

1. In a saucepan heat the oil and cook the mince for 5 minutes stirring, until lightly browned.
2. Turn the mixture into an ovenproof baking dish. Add the diced vegetables, and broth. Mix well.
3. Cover and bake for 30 minutes. Sprinkle the gelatine into the hot mixture.
4. Mix in the macaroni. Bake for a further 15 minutes. Stir well.
5. Cool 30 minutes before serving.

Refrigerated Storage

Store leftovers covered for maximum 1 week in refrigerator.

MINCE BAKED WITH VEGGIES AND QUINOA

Ingredients

- 500g pork or beef mince
- 2 cups (270g) carrots sliced
- ½ cup (80g) peas
- 1 cup (115g) butternut diced
- 1 cup (180g) quinoa
- 2¼ cups (560ml) broth
- g (1 tbsp) gelatine
- 25 ml oil (2 tbsp) vegetable oil

Instructions

1. Preheat the oven to 180C (350F).
2. In a saucepan heat the oil then add the mince. Cook for 5 minutes stirring, until lightly browned.
3. Turn the mixture into an ovenware baking dish. Add the broth, carrots, butternut and quinoa.
4. Cover and bake at 180C (350F) for 30 minutes or until all the liquid is absorbed. Stir well.
5. Sprinkle the gelatine into the hot mixture. Mix well.
6. Add peas and bake for a further 5 minutes. Cool before serving.

Refrigerated Storage

Store leftovers covered for maximum 1 week in refrigerator.

Freezer Storage

Store in freezer-safe containers or Ziplock bags max. 3 months.

Molly enjoys Beef Mince baked with Veggies & Quinoa

MINCE WITH VEGGIES AND COUSCOUS

Ingredients

- 500g pork or beef mince
- 1½ cups (175g) pumpkin diced
- ½ cup (100g) sweet potato diced
- cup (100g) diced celery
- 1½ cups (375ml) broth
- 1 tbsp (10g) unflavored gelatine
- 1 cup (190g) couscous
- 2 tbsp (25ml) vegetable oil

Note: *Some dogs may be allergic to the gluten in couscous. If your dog is prone to allergies, consult your veterinarian.*

Instructions

1. Wash, peel and slice the raw vegetables.
2. In a saucepan, heat the oil, stir in the mince and cook for 5 minutes or until lightly browned.
3. Add the beef broth, and gelatine and bring to the boil.
4. Add the prepared vegetables, cover and simmer for 35 minutes, stir well.
5. Stir the couscous into the hot mixture, then switch off the heat, cover and leave for 15 minutes to absorb the liquid. Stir well.
6. Allow to cool 30 minutes before serving.

Refrigerated / Freezer Storage

Store leftovers covered for maximum 1 week in refrigerator. Store in freezer-safe containers or Ziplock bags max. 3 months.

MINCE & VEGGIE HOTPOT

Ingredients

- 500g pork or beef mince
- 1 cup (140g) butternut diced
- 1½ cups (300g) raw sweet potato sliced
- ½ cup (80g) green peas
- ½ cup (75g) red bell peppers chopped
- 10g (1tbsp) unflavored gelatine
- 1½ cups (375ml) broth
- 1 tablespoon (15ml) vegetable oil

Instructions

1. Wash, peel and slice the raw vegetables.
2. In a saucepan, heat the oil, stir in the mince and cook for 5 minutes or until lightly browned.
3. Add the broth, and gelatine and bring to the boil.
4. Add the prepared vegetables, cover and simmer for 35 minutes, stir well. Cool before serving.

Refrigerated Storage

Store leftovers for maximum 1 week in refrigerator.

Freezer Storage

Freeze in airtight contained for up to 3 months. Once defrosted, store in refrigerator for maximum 2 days.

9. RECIPES FOR HEALTHY MEALS WITH LEAN BEEF OR CHICKEN HEART

What's included:

1. Beef Heart with Veggies & Couscous
2. Beef & Veggie Extravaganza
3. Beef Heart, Veggies & Pasta
4. Beef Heart & Veggie Casserole

Simple and inexpensive to prepare using readily available ingredients.

Meals made with lean beef heart are quick to make and not expensive. Your four-legged friends will beg for more.

These healthy meals will supplement the food you feed your dog with the protein, vitamins and minerals every dog needs to stay healthy and live a long, happy life.

Good plan to save time - prepare the broth in advance

It is a good plan to prepare and freeze the broth in advance, as this will save time when preparing the kibble replacement meals

Health Benefits

Beef heart is a nutritious source of protein needed to build healthy coat, skin, muscles, tendons and cartilage.

Note: *Some dogs may be allergic to the protein in beef and to gelatine.*

Portion sizes – A guideline only

The number of servings you will give your own dog to eat will depend on the size and breed of your pet, and how active your dog is.

Portion sizes listed for healthy meals in this recipe book are a guideline only, based on the approximate quantity my own dogs eat at each meal. That is, approximately 3-4 heaped tablespoons cooked food for each dog, per kibble replacement meal.

BEEF HEART WITH VEGGIES AND COUSCOUS

Ingredients

- 500g beef heart (or beef flank) cut into cubes
- 1½ cups (210g) butternut diced
- 1 cup (150g) green beans chopped
- 1½ cups (375ml) broth
- 1 cup (190g) couscous.
- 12ml (2 tbs) vegetable oil

Note: *Some dogs may be allergic to the gluten in couscous. If your dog is prone to allergies, consult your veterinarian.*

Instructions

1. In a saucepan heat the oil. Add the cubed beef and brown.
2. Add the broth and bring to a boil.
3. Add the vegetables.
4. Cook on medium for 40 minutes. Stir well.
5. Stir the couscous into the hot mixture, then switch off the heat, cover and leave for 15 minutes to absorb the liquid. Stir well.
6. Allow to cool 30 minutes before serving.

Refrigerated Storage

Store leftovers covered for maximum 1 week in refrigerator.

Freezer Storage

Store in freezer-safe containers or Ziplock bags max. 3 months.

BEEF HEART, VEGGIES & PASTA

Ingredients

- 500g beef heart
- cup (135g) carrots diced
- cup (1 medium) chopped sweet potato chopped
- ½ cup sugar snap peas sliced
- 2 cups (500ml) broth
- 1 cup macaroni
- 1 tbsp (25ml) vegetable oil

Instructions

1. In a saucepan heat the oil and cook the cubed hearts heat for 5 minutes stirring, until lightly browned.
2. Turn the mixture into an ovenproof baking dish. Add the diced vegetables, and broth. Mix well.
3. Cover and bake for 30 minutes at 180C (350F).
4. Mix in the macaroni. Bake for a further 15 minutes. Stir well.
5. Cool for 30 minutes before serving.

Refrigerated Storage

Store leftovers covered for maximum 1 week in refrigerator.

BEEF & VEGGIE EXTRAVAGANZA

Ingredients

- 500g lean beef, cubed
- 1 cup (135g) carrots sliced
- 1 cup (200g) celery sliced
- 1 cup (140g) butternut sliced
- 2 cups (500ml) broth
- ¾ cup (135g) quinoa
- 15ml vegetable oil

Instructions

1. Preheat the oven to 180C (350F).
2. In a saucepan heat the oil then add the cubed beef heart (or flank). Cook for 5 minutes stirring, until lightly browned. Mix well.
3. Turn the mixture into an ovenware baking dish. Add the broth, quinoa and vegetables.
4. Cover and bake for 30 minutes on low heat or until all the liquid is absorbed. Allow to cool before serving.

Refrigerated Storage

Store leftovers covered for maximum 1 week in refrigerator.

Freezer Storage

Store in freezer-safe containers or Ziplock bags for max. 3 months. Once defrosted, store in the refrigerator.

Beef & Veggie Extravaganza

TINKER'S BEST BEEF & VEGGIE CASSEROLE

Ingredients

- 500g cubed beef heart (or flank)
- cup (135g) carrots sliced
- 1½ cups (300g) raw sweet potato sliced
- ½ cup (75g) red bell peppers chopped
- 10g (1tbsp) unflavored gelatine
- 1½ cups (375ml) broth
- 1 tablespoon (15ml) cooking oil

Instructions

1. Wash, peel and slice the raw vegetables.
2. In a saucepan, heat the oil, stir in the beef and cook for 5 minutes or until lightly browned.
3. Add the beef broth, and gelatine and bring to the boil. Simmer on medium heat for 25 minutes. Sprinkle the gelatine into the hot mixture. Stir well to dissolve the gelatine.
4. Add the prepared vegetables, cover and simmer on medium heat for 10 minutes, stir well.
5. Cool before serving.

Refrigerated Storage

Store leftovers for maximum 1 week in refrigerator.

Freezer Storage

Freeze in airtight contained for up to 3 months. Once defrosted, store in refrigerator for maximum 2 days.

10. HEALTHY KIBBLE REPLACEMENT RECIPES WITH CHICKEN GIBLETS

What's included:

1. Bruno's Chicken Licken Giblets and Veggies
2. Slow-Cooked Chicken Giblets with Couscous
3. Misty's Favorite Chicken Giblets and Quinoa Bake
4. Chicken Giblets or Necks and Veggies with Rice
5. Chicken Giblets and Pasta Extraordinaire

Readily available ingredients. Simple to prepare and not expensive

Your furry friends will enjoy these delicious kibble replacement meals. Meals made with chicken necks, giblets and vegetables will supplement the food you feed your dog with the nutritious proteins, vitamins and minerals every dog needs to maintain health. It is a good plan to prepare and freeze the broth in advance, as this will save time when preparing the kibble replacement meals.

Health Benefits

Chicken is a nutritious source of protein needed to build healthy coat, skin and bones. ***Note:*** *Some dogs may be allergic to chicken and gelatine.*

Portion sizes – A guideline only

The number of servings you will give your own dog to eat will depend on the size and breed of your pet, and how active your dog is. Portion sizes listed for healthy meals in this recipe book are a guideline only, based on the approximate quantity my own dogs eat at each meal. That is, approximately 3-4 heaped tablespoons cooked food per kibble replacement meal.

Bruno's Chicken Licken Chicken Giblets & Veggies

BRUNO'S CHICKEN LICKEN GIBLETS & VEGGIES

Ingredients

- 500g chicken giblets
- 2 cups (270g) carrots sliced
- 1 cup (140g) butternut chopped
- ¾ cup (150g) raw sweet potato sliced
- ½ cup (75g) green beans chopped
- 10g (1tbsp) unflavored gelatine
- 1½ cups (375ml) chicken broth
- 1 tablespoon (15ml) vegetable oil

Instructions

1. Wash, peel and slice the raw vegetables.
2. In a saucepan, heat the oil, stir in the beef and cook for 5 minutes or until lightly browned.
3. Add the broth, and gelatine and bring to the boil. Turn down the heat and simmer for 35 minutes. Stir regularly.
4. Add the prepared vegetables, cover and simmer for 5-6 minutes on medium heat.
5. Cool before serving.

Refrigerated Storage

Store leftovers for maximum 1 week in refrigerator

Frozen Storage

Freeze in freezer proof containers or Ziplock bags for maximum 3 months. Once defrosted, store in refrigerator for maximum 2 days.

SLOW-COOKED CHICKEN GIBLETS WITH COUSCOUS

Ingredients

- 500g chicken giblets chopped
- 1½ cups (300g) sweet potato diced
- 1 cup (160g) peas
- ½ cup (75g) diced butternut
- 1 small tomato chopped.
- 1½ cups (375ml) broth
- 1 cup (190g) couscous.
- 12ml (2 tbsp) vegetable oil

Note: *Some dogs may be allergic to the gluten in couscous. If your dog is prone to allergies, consult your veterinarian.*

Instructions

1. In a saucepan bring the broth to a boil.
2. Combine the chopped giblets and vegetables in the slow cooker pot.
3. Stir in the boiling broth and cook on high for 20 minutes. Stir well. Then reduce the temperature to low heat for 1 hour.
4. Stir the couscous into the hot mixture, then switch off the slow cooker, cover and leave for 15 minutes to absorb the liquid. Stir well. Allow to cool 30 minutes before serving.

Refrigerated / Freezer Storage

Store leftovers for maximum 1 week in refrigerator.
Freeze in freezer proof containers or Ziplock bags for maximum 3 months. Once defrosted, store in refrigerator for maximum 2 days.

MISTY'S FAVORITE CHICKEN GIBLETS AND QUINOA BAKE

Ingredients

- 500g chicken giblets chopped
- 2 cups (60g) raw spinach chopped
- 1 cup (150g) carrots diced
- 1 cup (150g) celery sliced
- 1 cup (150g) butternut diced
- 2 cups (500ml) broth
- ½ cup (90g) quinoa
- 10g (1 tbsp) unflavored gelatine
- 10ml vegetable oil

Instructions

1. Preheat the oven to 180C (350F).
2. In a saucepan heat the oil then add the chopped chicken or turkey breast. Cook for 5 minutes stirring until lightly browned. Mix well.
3. Turn the mixture into an ovenware baking dish. Add the broth, quinoa and vegetables.
4. Cover and bake for 35 minutes on low heat or until the liquid is absorbed. Stir well. Sprinkle the gelatine into the hot mixture. Mix well.
5. Allow to cool before serving.

Refrigerated / Freezer Storage

Store leftovers for maximum 1 week in refrigerator.
Freeze in freezer proof containers or Ziplock bags for maximum
3 months. Once defrosted, store in refrigerator for maximum 2 days.

CHICKEN GIBLETS OR NECKS AND VEGGIES WITH RICE

Ingredients

- 500g chicken chopped giblets or necks
- 1 cup (115g) pumpkin sliced
- ½ cup (75g) carrot sliced
- ½ cup (80g) green peas
- 1 cup (200g) celery sliced
- 2 cups (500ml) broth
- ½ cup (90g) rice
- 10g (1tbsp) unflavored gelatine
- 10ml olive oil

Instructions

1. In a saucepan heat the oil then add the chopped chicken giblets. Cook for 5 minutes stirring until lightly browned.
2. Add the broth.
3. Cover and cook for 15 minutes on low heat. Sprinkle the gelatine into the hot mixture. Stir well to dissolve completely.
4. Add the rice and vegetables. cook for 20 minutes on low heat. Stir well.
5. Allow to cool before serving.

Refrigerated / Freezer Storage

Store leftovers for maximum 1 week in refrigerator.

Freeze in freezer proof containers or Ziplock bags for maximum 3 months. Once defrosted, store in refrigerator for maximum 2 days.

CHICKEN GIBLETS AND PASTA EXTRAORDINAIRE

Ingredients

- 500g chopped chicken giblets
- 1 cup (115g) pumpkin diced
- 1½ cups (150g) sweet potato diced
- 1 cup (180g) zucchini sliced
- 2 cups (500ml) chicken broth
- 1 cup macaroni
- ½ cup (125ml) plain yogurt
- 10g (1 tbs) unflavored gelatine
- 25ml (1 tbs) vegetable oil

Instructions

1. In a saucepan heat the oil and cook the cubed chicken or turkey breast for 5 minutes stirring until lightly browned.
2. Turn the mixture into an ovenproof baking dish. Add the diced vegetables, and broth. Mix well.
3. Cover and bake for 30 minutes at 180C (350F).
4. Sprinkle the gelatine into the mixture.
5. Mix in the macaroni and yogurt. Bake for a further 15 minutes.
6. Cool 30 minutes before serving.

Refrigerated Storage

Store leftovers covered for maximum 1 week in refrigerator.

11. HEALTHY KIBBLE REPLACEMENT MEALS – WITH LAMB

What's included:

1. Mutton Marrow Bone Broth
2. Teddy's Best Lamb and Quinoa Bowl
3. Lamb and Pasta Bake
4. Lamb Heart with Carrots, Peas and Rice
5. Teddy's Favorite Lamb Shoulder and Veggie Fiesta
6. Lamb with Couscous and Veggies

Fast and easy to prepare

Your furry friends will thoroughly enjoy these yummy homemade meals made with lamb (and/or mutton). Lamb and vegetables will supplement the food you feed your dog with the protein, vitamins and minerals every dog needs to live a long and healthy life.

Prepare the Broth in Advance

It will save time when cooking daily meals, if you prepare and freeze the broth in advance Chicken broth can be used to substitute the recipe for mutton marrow bone broth included in this section.

Health Benefits

Lamb (or mutton) Beef is a nutritious source of protein needed to build healthy coat, skin, muscles, tendons and cartilage.

> **Note**: *Some dogs may be allergic to the protein in lamb and to gelatine.*

Portion sizes – A guideline only

The number of servings you will give your own dog to eat will depend on the size and breed of your pet, and how active your dog is.

Portion sizes listed for healthy meals in this recipe book are a guideline only, based on the approximate quantity my own dogs eat at each meal. That is, approximately 3-4 heaped tablespoons of cooked food per kibble replacement meal.

HOMEMADE MUTTON MARROW BONE BROTH

Ingredients

- 1 kg meaty mutton marrow bones
- 3 chopped carrots
- 2 celery stalks chopped
- ½ cup chopped parsley
- 8 cups (2 liters) water

Note: Never feed cooked marrow bones to your furry companion.

Instructions

Option 1. Cook 1½ hour in Pressure Cooker

1. Place the raw bones, prepared vegetables and water in the pressure cooker.
2. Bring to the boil and simmer for 1½ hours on low heat.
3. Strain the broth. Discard the cooked marrowbones.

Option 2. Cook 3 hours in Slow Cooker

1. Place the raw bones, prepared vegetables and boiling water in the slow cooker.
2. Allow to cook for 3 hours on low heat.
3. Strain the broth. Discard the cooked marrowbones
4. Serve the cooked vegetables to supplement a meal.

Refrigerated / Frozen Storage

Cool broth. Store in glass canning jars in refrigerator. Max. 1 week. Freeze in freezer proof containers or Ziplock bags for maximum 3 months.

TEDDY'S BEST LAMB AND QUINOA BOWL

Ingredients

- 500g lamb heart (or boneless lamb shoulder) cubed
- 2 cups (60g) raw spinach chopped
- 1 cup (200g) sweet potato diced
- 1 cup (100g) celery sliced
- 1 cup (140g) butternut diced
- ½ cup (80g) green peas
- 2 cups (500ml) broth
- ½ cup (90g) quinoa
- 10g (1 tbsp) unflavored gelatine
- 2 tbsp (25ml) vegetable oil

Instructions

1. Preheat the oven to 180C (350F).
2. In a saucepan heat the oil then add the cubed lamb heart (or boneless shoulder). Cook for 5 minutes stirring, until lightly browned.
3. Turn the mixture into an ovenware baking dish. Add the broth, quinoa and vegetables.
4. Cover and bake for 35 minutes on low heat or until all the liquid is absorbed. Stir well. Sprinkle the gelatine into the hot mixture.
5. Allow to cool before serving.

Refrigerated /Freezer Storage

Store leftovers covered for maximum 1 week in refrigerator. Store in freezer-safe containers or Ziplock bags max. 3 months.

LAMB AND PASTA BAKE

Ingredients

- 500g lamb heart (or boneless shoulder) cut into cubes
- 1 cup (160g) potato diced
- 1 cup (135g) carrots diced
- 1 cup (180g) zucchini sliced
- 1 small tomato chopped
- 2 cups (500ml) mutton (or chicken) broth
- 1 cup macaroni
- 20ml yogurt
- 25ml (1 tbs) vegetable oil

Instructions

1. In a saucepan heat the oil and cook the cubed lamb for 5 minutes stirring until lightly browned.
2. Turn the mixture into an ovenproof baking dish. Add the diced vegetables, and broth. Mix well.
3. Cover and bake for 30 minutes.
4. Mix in the macaroni. Bake for a further 15 minutes. Stir well.
5. Cool 30 minutes before serving.

Refrigerated Storage

Store leftovers covered for maximum 1 week in refrigerator.

TEDDY'S FAVORITE LAMB SHOULDER & VEGGIE FIESTA

Ingredients

- 500g boneless lamb shoulder (or heart) cubed
- 1 cup (135g) carrots sliced
- 1 cup (200g) sweet potato diced
- ½ cup (75g) red bell peppers chopped
- 1 tbsp (10g) unflavored gelatine
- 1½ cups (375ml) broth
- 1 tbsp (15ml) cooking oil

Instructions

1. Wash, peel and slice the raw vegetables.
2. In a saucepan, heat the oil, stir in the lamb and cook for 5 minutes or until lightly browned.
3. Add the beef broth, and gelatine and bring to the boil.
4. Add the prepared vegetables, cover and simmer for 35 minutes, stir well.
5. Cool before serving.

Refrigerated Storage

Store leftovers for maximum 1 week in refrigerator.

Freezer Storage

Freeze in airtight contained for up to 3 months. Once defrosted, store in refrigerator for maximum 2 days.

LAMB HEART WITH CARROTS, PEAS AND RICE

Ingredients

- 500g lamb heart (or boneless shoulder) cut into cubes
- 3 cups (400g) carrots sliced
- ½ cup (80g) peas
- 1 cup (250ml) broth
- ½ cup (90g) rice
- 1 tbsp (10g) unflavored gelatine
- 2 tbsp (25ml) olive oil

Instructions

1. In a saucepan bring the lamb and broth to the boil. Simmer for 15 minutes on low heat.
2. Add the rice and carrots and cook for a further 20 minutes on low heat.
3. Sprinkle the gelatine into the mixture and stir well, to dissolve the gelatine.
4. Stir in the peas and cook for a further 5 minutes.
5. Allow to cool before serving.

Refrigerated Storage

Store leftovers covered for maximum 1 week in refrigerator.

Freezer Storage

Store in freezer-safe containers or Ziplock bags max. 3 months.

Lamb with Carrots, Peas and Rice

LAMB WITH COUSCOUS AND VEGGIES

Ingredients

- 500g lamb heart (or boneless shoulder) cut into cubes
- 1½ cups (175g) pumpkin diced
- ½ cup (80g) potatoes diced
- ½ cup (90g) broccoli, finely chopped
- 1½ cups (375ml) broth
- 1 cup (190g) couscous.
- 25ml (2 tbsp) vegetable oil

Note: *Some dogs may be allergic to the gluten in couscous. If your dog is prone to allergies, consult your veterinarian.*

Instructions

1. In a saucepan heat the oil.
2. Then add the lamb and cook stirring for 5 minutes or until lightly browned.
3. Add the broth and bring to a boil. Turn down the heat, cover and simmer covered for 25 minutes.
4. Add the vegetables and cook for 10 minutes.
5. Stir the couscous into the hot mixture. Bring to the boil, then cover and allow to stand for 15 minutes to absorb the liquid. Stir well.
6. Allow to cool 30 minutes before serving.

Refrigerated / Freezer Storage

Store leftovers covered for maximum 1 week in refrigerator.
Store in freezer-safe containers or Ziplock bags max. 3 months.

12. HEALTHY KIBBLE REPLACEMENT RECIPES COOKED WITH LIVER

What's included:

1. Liver Extravaganza with Quinoa
2. Liver with Couscous
3. Snoopy's Favorite Liver & Veggies
4. Liver and Pumpkin Medley with Rice
5. Liver and Veggie Hotpot

Readily available ingredients, simple to prepare

These relatively inexpensive kibble replacement meals made with liver are quick and easy to prepare. You can choose to use either beef, mutton, or chicken livers. Your dogs will beg for more.

Healthy kibble replacement meals made with liver will supplement the food you feed your dog with the protein, vitamins and minerals every dog needs to live a long and healthy life.

It is a good plan to prepare and freeze the broth in advance, as this will save time when preparing the kibble replacement meals.

Health Benefits

Liver is a highly nutritious source of protein needed to build healthy coat, skin, muscles, and bones.

Note *Some dogs may be allergic to liver and to gelatine.*

Portion sizes – A guideline only

The number of servings you will give your own dog to eat will depend on the size and breed of your pet, and how active your dog is.

Portion sizes listed for healthy meals in this recipe book are a guideline only, based on the approximate quantity my own dogs eat at each meal. That is, approximately 3 -4 heaped tablespoons cooked food per kibble replacement meal.

Liver Extravaganza with Quinoa

LIVER EXTRAVAGANZA WITH QUINOA

Ingredients

- 500g liver (beef, lamb or chicken)
- 2 cups (260g) carrots diced
- 1 cup (150g) celery sliced
- 3/4 cup (100g) butternut diced
- ½ cup (80g) peas
- 2 cups (500ml) broth
- ¾ cup (135g) quinoa
- 1 tbsp (10g) unflavored gelatine
- 10ml vegetable oil

Instructions

1. Preheat the oven to 180C (350F).
2. In a saucepan heat the oil then add the chopped liver. Cook for 5 minutes stirring until lightly browned.
3. Turn the mixture into an ovenware baking dish. Add the broth, quinoa, carrots, celery and butternut.
4. Cover and bake for 30 minutes on low heat or until all the liquid is absorbed. Stir well. Sprinkle the gelatine into the hot mixture. Mix well.
5. Stir in the peas. Bake for 5 minutes.
6. Allow to cool before serving.

Refrigerated / Freezer Storage

Cool the broth then store in glass canning jars in refrigerator. Max.1 week.

Freeze in freezer proof containers or Ziplock bags for maximum 3 months.

LIVER WITH COUSCOUS

Ingredients

- 500g liver (beef, lamb or chicken) cubed
- 1½ cups (210g) diced butternut
- ½ cup (100g) sweet potato diced
- 1 cup (30g) chopped spinach
- 1½ cups (375ml) broth
- 1 tbsp (10g) unflavored gelatine
- 1 cup (190g) couscous
- 12ml (2 tbs) vegetable oil

Note: Some dogs may be allergic to the gluten in couscous. If your dog is prone to allergies, consult your veterinarian.

Instructions

1. In a saucepan heat the oil, then add the liver and cook stirring to lightly brown.
2. Add the broth and bring to a boil. Add the vegetables.
3. Simmer for 20 minutes. Stir well. Sprinkle the gelatine into the hot mixture.
4. Stir the couscous into the hot mixture, then switch off the heat, cover the saucepan and leave for 15 minutes to absorb the liquid. Stir well.
5. Allow to cool 30 minutes before serving.

Refrigerated / Freezer Storage

Store leftovers covered for maximum 1 week in refrigerator.
Store in freezer-safe containers or Ziplock bags max. 3 months.

SNOOPY'S FAVORITE LIVER & VEGGIES

Ingredients

- 500g liver (beef, lamb or chicken) cubed
- ¾ cup (125g) chopped celery
- 1½ cups (210g) butternut diced
- 1 cup (180g) zucchini sliced
- 2 cups (500ml) broth
- 1 cup macaroni
- 1 tbsp (10g) unflavored gelatine
- 1 tbsp (25ml) vegetable oil

Instructions

1. In a saucepan heat the oil and cook the liver for 5 minutes stirring, until lightly browned.
2. Turn the mixture into an ovenproof baking dish. Add the diced vegetables, and broth. Mix well.
3. Cover and bake for 30 minutes. Sprinkle the gelatine into the hot mixture.
4. Mix in the macaroni. Bake for a further 15 minutes. Stir well.
5. Cool for 30 minutes before serving.

Refrigerated Storage

Store leftovers covered for maximum 1 week in the refrigerator.

LIVER AND PUMPKIN MEDLEY WITH RICE

Ingredients

- 500g liver (beef, lamb or chicken) chopped
- ½ cup (70g) pumpkin sliced
- ½ cup (75g) green beans
- ½ cup (75g) celery chopped
- 2 cups (500ml) broth
- ½ cup (90g) rice
- 10ml vegetable oil

Instructions

1. In a saucepan heat the oil then add the chopped (chicken or beef or lamb) liver. Cook for 5 minutes stirring, until lightly browned.
2. Add vegetables, rice and broth
3. Cover and cook 35 minutes on low heat. Stir well. Add more water if needed.
4. Allow to cool before serving.

Refrigerated Storage

Store leftovers covered for maximum 1 week in refrigerator.

Freezer Storage

Store in freezer-safe containers or Ziplock bags max. 3 months.

LIVER & VEGGIE HOTPOT

Ingredients

- 500g liver (beef, lamb or chicken) cubed
- 1 cup (115g) pumpkin chopped
- 1 cup (160g) diced potato
- ½ cup (60g) red bell peppers chopped
- ½ cup (75g) cabbage chopped
- 1½ cups (375ml) broth
- 1 tbsp (10g) unflavored gelatine
- 2 tbsp (25ml) cooking oil

Instructions

1. Wash, peel and slice the raw vegetables.
2. In a saucepan, heat the oil and stir in the liver. Cook for 5 minutes stirring well.
3. Stir in the broth and vegetables. Bring to the boil, cover and simmer for 30 minutes.
4. Add the prepared vegetables and bring to the boil. Simmer for 10 minutes, stir well.
5. Cool before serving.

Refrigerated Storage

Store leftovers for maximum 1 week in refrigerator.

Freezer Storage

Freeze in airtight contained for up to 2 months. Once defrosted, store in refrigerator for maximum 2 days.

13. HELPFUL TIPS - FOODS TO AVOID AND FOODS SAFE TO EAT

Before introducing kibble replacement meals, it's a good plan to familiarize yourself about foods that are safe for your dog to eat and foods to avoid.

Some of the Foods to Avoid feeding your Dog

Contact your veterinarian if you suspect your dog has eaten any of the foods listed below.

- **Avocado** can cause diarrhea, vomiting and heart congestion. If your dog ate a small piece of avocado, it will be okay, but ensure you monitor your dog for any symptoms

- **Almonds, pecans, and walnuts** contain high amounts of oils and fats that can cause vomiting and diarrhea, and potentially pancreatitis in pets.

- **Alcohol**: never give your dog food or beverages containing alcohol can cause vomiting, central nervous system failure, difficulty breathing, coma and death.

- **Chocolate, Coffee and Caffeine** are highly toxic to dogs. When eaten, can cause vomiting and diarrhea, panting, abnormal heart rhythm, seizures and even death.

- **Garlic onions, leeks, and chives** are toxic to dogs. Side effects include anemia, pale gums, elevated heart rate, weakness, and collapse. Poisoning may have delayed symptoms, so monitor your dog for several days.

- **Grapes and Raisins** contain tartaric acid which is toxic to dogs. As dogs can't excrete tartaric acid, it can cause kidney failure.

- **Macadamia Nuts** can cause weakness, depression, vomiting, tremors and hyperthermia in dogs. Signs usually appear within 12 hours of ingestion and can last approximately 24 to 48 hours.

- **Raw Eggs** can contain harmful bacteria, such as salmonella and e coli that cause diarrhea. The raw egg white contains avidin, which prevents absorption of Biotin, a B vitamin, leading to skin and coat problems.

- **Raw Yeast Dough** can cause a dog's stomach to bloat and potentially twist, becoming a life- threatening emergency.

- **Salt and Salty Snack Foods** - Eating too much salt can produce excessive thirst and urination, or even sodium ion poisoning in pets. Eating too many salty foods can cause vomiting, diarrhea, depression, tremors, elevated body temperature, seizures and even death.

This content has been adapted from the article 'People Foods to Avoid Feeding Your Pets' published by ASPCA Animal Poison Control Centre.

Foods That Are Safe for Dogs to Eat

On a personal level: We feed our dogs (including adult dogs) Royal Canin Puppy Medium dog food, which contains 32% protein. In addition, we supplement daily with homemade treats, and 3 times weekly, with 1 kibble replacement meal. We have no obese dogs and no dogs with chronic illnesses.

- **Eggs**: Cooked eggs are safe for dogs and are an excellent source of protein.
- **Cashews**: A few unsalted cashews at a time make a healthy treat. Cashews contain proteins, fat, calcium and magnesium.
- **Cheese**: Dogs can eat cheese in small to moderate quantities, provided the dog isn't lactose intolerant, which is rare. Cheese can be a healthy treat.
- **Corn**: Corn is one of the most common ingredients in most dog foods and is safe for dogs to eat. But avoid corn on the cob, as there is a risk that it can cause an intestinal blockage.
- **Cow's Milk** is safe for dogs to drink in small quantities and is an excellent source of calcium and protein. However, some dogs may be lactose intolerant.
- **Fish**: Dogs can eat cooked fish. Salmon and sardines are rich in proteins, good fats and vitamins.
- **Meat**: Beef, lamb, pork etc. are safe for dogs to eat, provided the meat is thoroughly cooked to destroy harmful bacteria, such as E. coli and salmonella, which cause serious infections.
- **Oats**: Yes, in moderation, cooked, unflavored oatmeal and oats are not toxic to dogs and are a rich source of fiber, vitamins and minerals. Although oats is a healthy supplement, avoid giving your dog more than 20g of oats per day, as overfeeding can cause bloat or diarrhea. Some dogs may be allergic to oats.

Foods that are safe for dogs to eat

- **Peanut butter**: Natural peanut butter with no added sugar or salt is an excellent source of protein for dogs. It contains heart-healthy fats, vitamins B and E and niacin.

- **Peanuts**: Unsalted peanuts in moderation are safe for dogs to eat. They are rich in good fats and proteins.
- **Poultry**: Yes, cooked chicken, duck & turkey are safe for dogs to eat. Avoid giving bones which can splinter and cause intestinal blockage.
- **Quinoa**: Yes, quinoa is safe for dogs to eat. It is a healthy alternative to wheat and corn.
- **Vegetables:** The following are just some of the vegetables that are safe for dogs to eat in moderation. Vegetables supplement the food you feed your dogs with fiber, vitamins and minerals:
    - Cabbage
    - Broccoli
    - Cauliflower
    - Sweet Potato
    - Potatoes
    - Carrots
    - Pumpkin
    - Peas
    - Green Beans
    - Zucchini
    - Sweet Bell Peppers.
- **Wheat/grains**: Yes, wheat and other grains are safe for dogs to eat. Wheat and corn are good sources of protein, essential fatty acids, and fiber. If your dog is prone to allergies, consult your veterinarian for recommendations.
- **Yogurt**: Plain, unsweetened yogurt is safe for dogs to eat. Avoid any yogurts with added sugar and skip all yogurt with artificial sweeteners.

This information has been adapted from "People Food Dogs Can Eat and Can't Eat – American Kennel Club" by AKC Staff 14 March 2024.

14. TIPS ON TRAINING YOUR DOG WITH HEALTHY REWARD-TREATS & SNACKS

Positive Reward-Training Using Homemade Treats

Positive reward-training is a great way to bond with your four-legged friends and ensure that they quickly learn to obey your instructions. I hope you will find my insights below helpful.

When you reward your dog with a delicious home-made treat that he/she enjoys eating, your furry friend is likely to repeat the behavior going forward. Equally, if your dog dislikes the way you go about training it, your behavior will negatively impact your dog's desire to repeat the required behavior.

That's why positive reward-training training using nutritious homemade treats is such an effective training tool.

Well-trained Jesse always obeys instructions

Step 1. Select a favorite snack or treat as the reward.

I personally find the soft, nutritious gelatin-based chewy treats I make (with chicken broth, unflavored gelatin and liquidized carrots or sweet potato) to be the reward-treats my dogs love best. Snacks made with chicken livers are second best on their list of favorites. As each dog is different, it's a good plan to always keep sufficient of their favorite reward-treats in stock.

Step 2. Establish a routine. Start with training to eliminate outside.

In general, my biggest concern is to ensure that my dogs learn to eliminate outside. I take my 8–12-week-old puppies out onto the grass as soon as they wake up, immediately after eating and generally every 1-2 hours. As soon as they have eliminated, I praise them enthusiastically, saying 'good dog' and reward with a favorite treat. You can use your own preferred words to praise your dog but use the same phrase each time. By the time they are 3 months old, my puppies are generally house trained.

Step 3. Training dogs to obey commands

Training your dog generally starts with basic commands such as 'sit', 'come', 'stay' and 'No'. The repetition of these simple words and rewarding them with healthy, homemade treats when they comply, helps to establish a positive relationship between you and your four-legged friend.

It's a good plan to teach your pet one command at a time, and to give a favorite reward snack or treat only once the dog has obeyed the instruction. Once your furry friend has learned to understand and obey a command, introduce the next command. Common instructions used to train dogs to obey include 'sit', 'wait', 'lie down', 'fetch', 'come', 'off', 'shake' and 'drop it'.

Step 4. What if your dog refuses to obey?

If you experience difficulties training your dog to obey, I strongly recommend that you consult an Animal Behaviorist, who can train you on how to train your dog. I learned everything I know about training my own dogs to obey, by taking a course in Animal Behavior conducted by a well-respected Animal Behaviorist.

I lie on my back when I don't want to listen.

REFERENCES

US Department of Agriculture (USDA) FoodData Central Website
https://fdc.nal.usda.gov/

The 8 Biggest Dog Food Myths by the American Kennel Club.
https://www.akc.org/expert-advice/nutrition/dog-food-myths/44

People Foods to Avoid Feeding Your Pets published by ASPCA Animal Poison Control Centre. https://www.aspca.org/pet-care/animal-poison-control/people-foods-avoid-feeding-your-pets

People Food Dogs Can Eat and Can't Eat – American Kennel Club" by AKC Staff 14 March, 2024
https://www.akc.org/expert-advice/nutrition/human-foods-dogs-can-and-cant-eat/

Basic Dog Feeding Guide
https://kb.rspca.org.au/knowledge-base/what-should-i-feed-my-dog/#basic-dog-feeding-guide

www.ingramcontent.com/pod-product-compliance
Lightning Source LLC
LaVergne TN
LVHW021714080426
835510LV00010B/992